Aylesbury
in the 1960s

A wet day in the High Street, before Jarvis's built its extension on to the block seen behind, 1963. (*M. Sale*)

BRITAIN IN OLD PHOTOGRAPHS

Aylesbury in the 1960s

KARL VAUGHAN

SUTTON PUBLISHING LIMITED

Sutton Publishing Limited
Phoenix Mill · Thrupp · Stroud
Gloucestershire · GL5 2BU

First published 2000

Copyright © Karl Vaughan, 2000

Half-title page photograph: Cottages in Green
End, just off Rickfords Hill.
Title page photograph: Shoppers in Market
Square, 1964.

British Library Cataloguing in Publication Data
A catalogue record for this book is available from the
British Library.

ISBN 0-7509-2383-0

Typeset in 10.5/13.5 Photina.
Typesetting and origination by
Sutton Publishing Limited.
Printed and bound in England
by J.H. Haynes & Co. Ltd, Sparkford.

The County Hall in Market Square seen from the office block in Friars Square, 1968. (*R.J. Johnson*)

CONTENTS

Bourbon Street, 1963. This row of buildings was to disappear in 1964 to make way for Friars Square. (*M. Sale*)

A view along Buckingham Street, 1963. It shows the old slaughterhouse awaiting demolition. (*M. Sale*)

INTRODUCTION

After my first book, *Aylesbury Past & Present*, was published, I was asked many times when I would compile another. I decided to do just that, but this time concentrating just on the period from 1960 up to 1969 using only old photographs. Soon after the first book was published, I discovered a collection of pictures that showed Aylesbury in the 1960s in great detail. And so another book was born.

The main ideas for the redevelopment of the town centre really originated in the 1930s when traffic first started to cause a problem. Various plans were put forward by the Borough Council to solve this, but proceedings were halted by the Second World War. When the war was over, the project was focused on again. Among the first of the plans was the idea for a southern approach road. This was to start from the Hartwell bend (where the roundabout for Ellen Road now is), cross the railway line by the station and continue along the line of Great Western Street. It was then to curve round into Walton Street and head out of the town centre. In conjunction with this plan was a scheme to widen the old Oxford Road all the way from the Hen & Chickens pub, up Rickfords Hill and down old Friarage Road to join with the proposed new junction with Walton Street and Great Western Street. The Public Baths in Bourbon Street and two pubs, the Falcon and the Greyhound in Great Western Street, were demolished so that these two projects could go ahead. Later on, though, the approach road scheme was dropped because of financial problems, and the other scheme was altered when Friars Square came along.

At the same time more housing was needed in Aylesbury because the town had to be ready to accommodate people moving from London. Housing estates, including Bedgrove, Quarrendon and Elmhurst, were built. To serve this growing population, it was decided that the town needed a new central shopping area. The Borough Council envisaged having everything under one roof. Shoppers could park their cars in a multi-storey car park, walk across a covered walkway and shop in a large open area and in a sheltered environment. After various plans had been pushed back and forth, Friars Square was born. The area that was to disappear in this development was the southern side of Bourbon Street, the bottom south-western side of Market Square, all the buildings in Great Western Street, Friarage Road, Silver Street with Silver Lane and a few buildings at the top of Walton Street. Many businesses were affected by this development. Where would they go? Many simply had to close, while others were offered new sites in Friars Square.

Another development under way just before Friars Square was the new County Offices and County Library in Walton Street. More of the old town had to be demolished to accommodate this huge building. The most unfortunate thing about all of this clearance is that no archaeological surveys were carried out. As is shown in this book, there were many buildings that were possibly 400 years or more old. The worst aspect of the redevelopment was all the deep excavation work. The natural gradient from Bourbon Street right down to Great Western Street was dug away and lost forever. Layers of the town's history disappeared in a few weeks. Apparently the excavation at the Bourbon Street end was as deep as 30 ft, which indicates just how much soil was carted away.

I have also included in this book a section on the pubs in the town in about 1962. Aylesbury has long been known for having a large number of pubs. Because the focus of the book is the 1960s, I am unable to include establishments such as the John Kennedy, the Buckinghamshire Yeoman, the new Hen & Chickens and the Dairy Maid, as these were all built a bit later. Many of the pubs shown have gone, but the town today still boasts over forty.

The 1960s saw the coldest winter in living memory, with frost temperatures said to be as low as 30 degrees below zero. Not only was it cold but there was also snow on the ground from December 1962 to March 1963. Of course there were problems with flooding when the thaw began. It must have been strange to see green grass again after such a long time. In the 1960s a good fall of snow every year was almost guaranteed, but now the winters are wetter and milder – possibly because of global warming.

The compilation of this book has been a very interesting project. The photographs used are mostly previously unpublished and are of a very high quality. I imagine that these images will jog a few memories for some people as well as providing a detailed insight into the profound changes that have occurred in Aylesbury.

Karl Vaughan
Summer 2000

1

The Beginning of the Decade

A sunny view of Market Square, 1960. (*M. Sale*)

We start the book with a photograph of a pub that stood in Walton Green. This was the original Plough & Harrow which is seen here in 1960 and by this time was closed. Just out of view to the left is the newer Old Plough & Harrow. The older building was demolished at about the time when the gyratory system opened in 1969. (*M. Sale*)

A busy Market Square in 1961. As can be seen, the middle of the square is quite full of cars which was not uncommon on non-market days. The empty space between Ashford's and the Midland Bank was occupied by Dewhurst the butcher's, and tobacconists Waters. Because of their premises being demolished, Waters moved to the bottom of Silver Street. (*M. Sale*)

Cambridge Street, 1961. These are the buildings that used to adjoin the Odeon and were probably built in Victorian times. The first was Janetta's, which sold ice creams and snacks; next is the Vale School of Motoring which by this time was closed. The more modern building on the left is part of the former Odeon cinema. In the distance is St John's Church. (*M. Sale*)

Another view of Cambridge Street, 1961. Taken from the entrance to Anchor Lane, this shows the two shops that were at the end of the row of buildings shown in the previous photograph. The shop on the left is the butcher's A.B. Deeley and on the right is Steggall's radio and electrical store. Originally there were three more properties joining these buildings; they were demolished in the early 1950s. (*M. Sale*)

The canal, photographed during the Boat Rally in August 1961. Organised by the Inland Waterways Association, this was the eighth National Rally of Boats which brought together vessels from such diverse places as Bridgwater in Somerset and Ripon in Yorkshire. The event lasted for five days. On the last day there was a dinner at the Bulls Head where trophies and prizes were awarded for the best-looking boats. (*M. Sale*)

Whitehall Street, 1961. This photograph was taken at the bottom of the street where it met White Hill, which is where the lorry is approaching from. This part of town included many old buildings. Note the one in the centre with the possibly Victorian façade. This road was very narrow, which posed a problem when two large vehicles needed to pass each other. These buildings have since been demolished, and White Hill is now a dual carriageway that passes through where they once stood. (*M. Sale*)

Another view of Whitehall Street, 1961. This photograph was taken from the entrance of Nelson Terrace which leads to the churchyard. As already mentioned, these buildings would soon be gone and were clearly in a dilapidated condition. Today a new wall replaces the original front garden walls seen here; beyond it is the dual carriageway of White Hill. (*M. Sale*)

Market Square, 1962. Demolition work is underway on Jones & Cocks ironmonger's shop. Round the corner from Weston's is Freeman Hardy & Willis's shoe shop which was soon to expand its premises to take in Weston's together with a new building that would occupy the site of Jones & Cocks. (*M. Sale*)

Looking down Great Western Street, April 1962. Here we see the Halton RAF apprentices' band marching round into Market Square in preparation for a visit from Queen Elizabeth II. Her Majesty spent three hours in the town and visited the Grange School where she had luncheon. Also on her way around the town, she visited the home of Mr and Mrs Powell at 142 Oxford Road. Imagine their shock to see the Queen coming up their path! Not something that happens every day of the week. (*B. Thorpe*)

Closed Market Street, August 1962. This shows the demolition of the buildings that were occupied by Adams the tobacconist and Marshall's bookshop. These buildings were said to be unsafe and were immediately shored up and eventually knocked down. While the site was being cleared it was asked whether Market Street could be widened or left as it was so that the Kings Head could be clearly seen. Neither of these ideas came to fruition and a new building was built on the site. (*M. Sale*)

Park Street footbridge, 1962. By this time the railway that it stood over served only goods trains, and in only a couple of years or so the rails were dismantled and the bridge taken down. Just beyond the bridge are houses in Stocklake which still exist today. (*R.W. Powell*)

Another photograph taken at the same time as the one above, but looking from the bridge itself – and what a view you get. In the centre a train is seen approaching from the coal sidings. The only tall buildings noticeable on the horizon are in the centre – the Congregational church in the High Street with Jarvis's new tower block just to the right of it. After the railway disappeared the site was waste ground for many years, until recently when it became Vale Retail Park. (*R.W. Powell*)

Firemen putting out a fire which was caused by a paraffin heater on the front seat of this Triumph sports car parked in Market Square, 1962. This photograph was loaned to me by the son of the fireman, who is seen here standing with his mother to the right of the picture. (*I. West*)

2

The Pubs of Aylesbury,
c. 1962

The sign of the Green Man in Market Square. (*M. Sale*)

The Star Hotel in Railway Street. Facing the entrance to Station Street, this handsome Victorian building was originally a coaching inn – which is indicated by the large entrance to the stables. Sadly, it was demolished in the early 1970s to make way for Hampden House. (*M. Sale*)

The Prince of Wales at the bottom of Station Street. This pub replaced an earlier building of the same name and stood opposite the Star Hotel. Originally this street had two other pubs, namely the Railway Tavern which is shown in the next chapter (*see* page 51) and The Ark at the top of the street. (*M. Sale*)

The Millwright's Arms in Walton Road, 1962. This too replaced an earlier building and looks remarkably similar in design to the Prince of Wales shown on the previous page. They were probably rebuilt at about the same time. (*M. Sale*)

The Ship in Walton Street. In early records this was known as the Jolly Bargeman, which seems a much more fitting name for the pub given its proximity to the canal. These days it stands almost on its own facing the dual carriageway that Walton Street has become. Going back many decades before the road widening, there used to be another pub opposite the Ship called the Anchor, but that has long since gone. (*M. Sale*)

One of the town's older pubs – the Harrow Inn, Buckingham Street. The doorway seen below the pub sign was originally part of a building that stood on the corner of Cambridge Street. It was pulled down to give traffic an easier view of Buckingham Street when approaching the junction. (*M. Sale*)

The Barley Corn in Cambridge Street is another very old pub and has some very low ceilings, which can be quite a hindrance if you're over 6 ft tall! This pub was joined with the Harrow in the early 1980s to become the Harrow & Barleycorn. Since then it has become the Farmyard & Firkin, owned by the Firkin Brewery which has many pubs up and down the country. (*M. Sale*)

The Plough in Tring Road. The licence for this pub was transferred from the original building that stood opposite the Royal Bucks Hospital. The old building was pulled down in about 1960. (*M. Sale*)

The Railway Hotel, Great Western Street. This pub was originally known as the New Railway Tavern and was a fairly plain building up until 1898, when it was modernized and embellished with just about every architectural feature that was in fashion at the time. The pub closed in December 1966 and, as is seen later in this book (*see* page 108), was demolished to make way for Friars Square. (*M. Sale*)

The Hop Pole in Bicester Road. This is one of the town's Victorian inns and has remained largely unchanged over the years. It is also renowned for being a popular venue for local bands. The street on the right is Southern Road, which is an industrial area. (*M. Sale*)

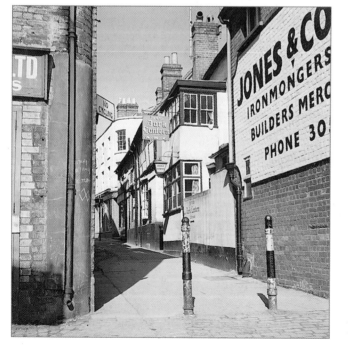

The Dark Lantern in Silver Street. This is another of the town's oldest pubs and has kept its name pretty much the same over the last few hundred years. On a map of 1809 it was known as The Lanthorn; it has now reverted to that name, although the spelling has altered. The building belonging to Jones & Cocks on the right has now become part of The Lantern. (*M. Sale*)

The Green Man in Market Square. In its handsome setting, this was one of eight pubs in the square. Since it closed in the early 1980s the property has undergone a number of name changes. After a short time as Saint's wine bar, it became to Butler's, a title it kept until 1999. It was then changed yet again to The Market Tavern – a more fitting name. (*M. Sale*)

The Derby Arms in St Mary's Square. This is an unusual looking building: its false Georgian façade has been added to a much older building – a feature that is quite common in Church Street, for example. The pub closed and has been turned into apartments. Its closure was a sad loss, but at least the building has been preserved, something which is rare in this town. (*M. Sale*)

The Rising Sun in Oxford Road. Another old pub, probably seventeenth or eighteenth century in date. This was one of those inns you stepped down into, and if you were quite tall you were more than likely bang your head on the way in! (*M. Sale*)

Walton Brewery in Walton Street. Not strictly a pub, this was the home of the Aylesbury Brewery Company, who owned many of the pubs in this chapter. The buildings seen here covered quite a large area and were demolished to make way for a modern 1960s building called Planar House. A view of this building is seen later on page 114. (*M. Sale*)

The Oddfellows' Arms in Cambridge Street. Here's another pub that's been around for a long time. It is rather an odd-shaped building, with its large sloping roof. It is the only surviving pre-Victorian building in this part of town. Just behind the pub is St John's Church, which was sadly demolished in 1970 to make way for the car park of the Telephone Exchange. (*M. Sale*)

The Hen & Chickens in Oxford Road. This is how the pub looked before it was rebuilt in 1966. It was given a full licence in 1958 and as part of the conditions for this the Plume of Feathers in Castle Street was closed. Sadly both of these buildings have since disappeared. (*M. Sale*)

The Horse and Jockey, Buckingham Road. At the time this photograph was taken, this was the first building you would come to as you approached Aylesbury from the north. This is no longer the case as the housing estates of Watermead and Elmhurst are in its immediate vicinity, which indicates how Aylesbury is slowly encroaching upon the countryside. There was also another pub called the Horse & Jockey, on the Wendover Road. A photograph of it is seen on page 42. (*M. Sale*)

The Two Brewers, Buckingham Street. The area at the rear of this pub was originally used for stabling. The shape of the doorway is similar in design to the one that was in the Prince of Wales pub in Station Street (*see* page 18). Both of these pubs have since been demolished. Offices and shops now occupy the site of the Two Brewers and its adjacent buildings, which have also been replaced. (*M. Sale*)

The Duck Inn, Camborne Avenue. This, the first of Bedgrove's pubs, was opened in December 1963. Judging by the newly planted trees this photograph must have been taken soon after that date. (*M. Sale*)

The New Zealand, Buckingham Road. Another of Aylesbury's Victorian pubs, it is seen here with its original brick front, which has since been painted over. On old maps this part of Buckingham Road was known as New Zealand. (*M. Sale*)

The Broad Leys, Wendover Road. The original name of this pub was the New Inn. Its name was changed in 1958 because it was no longer being used as an inn, and its status was changed to a pub. Ironically the pub is soon to become a motel, with a new bedroom block at the rear. (*M. Sale*)

The George, Market Square. This was a remnant of the well-known George Hotel, which stood where Burton's now is. Careful examination shows that there is still part of the old building left. Between the pub and Burton's is a very narrow bit of wall with two projecting bands of stone. These bands used to extend right across. When the old building was demolished it must have been safer to leave this wall there to protect the one next door. The George has now become a building society. (*M. Sale*)

The County Arms, Cambridge Street. Another Victorian pub, it looks much the same now as it did when this picture was taken. Webster & Cannon's brickyard was behind this pub, where Cambridge Close now is. The former brickyard is now full of retail units. (*M. Sale*)

The Windmill, Cambridge Street, had a distinctive frontage. The pub has since closed but the building still looks much the same. This together with the white building immediately on the left, is now part of Hampden Veterinary Surgery. The fenced area on the right was the garden of Hazells Club. The club was in Britannia Street and is seen on page 119. (*M. Sale*)

The Bricklayer's Arms, Walton Street. One of Aylesbury's smaller pubs it has some low ceilings and is timber-framed, which isn't obvious from its outward appearance. The pub is still open today and has retained its character. (*M. Sale*)

The Borough Arms, Park Street, 1962. The new pub shown here replaced the original building in 1959. The rebuilding was done to improve the junction with Bierton Road, so the new pub was built much further back. Over the years the pub has been extended a few times and is now known as The Weavers. (*M. Sale*)

The Old Plough & Harrow, Stoke Road. Behind here was another pub called the Plough & Harrow, which is seen on page 10. The old pub was demolished in about 1969 when the gyratory system was put in. Today the Old Plough & Harrow still exists, although it is now called the Whistling Duck – which is apparently a New Zealand bird. Whatever next?! (*M. Sale*)

The Victoria, Bourbon Street. Another of the town's smaller pubs, it has closed since this picture was taken. Today the building looks largely unchanged and retains its pub sign bracket. The Pound Shop now occupies the premises. (*M. Sale*)

The White Swan, Walton Street. One of Aylesbury's older pubs, it is timber-framed. It was also a coaching inn and had stable at the rear. Next to the Whit Swan on the left is the Bell Hotel. (*M. Sale*)

The Britannia, Buckingham Road. We see it here as it looked in its unpainted state. The narrow road on the righ is New Street. That road has changed vastly since this photo was taken, and is now about four times its origina width – something that is quite common in the town. (*M. Sale*)

The Saracens Head in Rickfords Hill. This old pub has had its façade altered, as have many of the buildings in this area. The building is probably seventeenth century in date. Today the pub still looks much the same as it did when this picture was taken. Thankfully this area was left pretty much alone during all the development. (*M. Sale*)

The King's Head, Market Square. This photograph shows how the pub looked after the demolition of the buildings that stood in front of it. At the time the Borough Council explored the possibility of keeping this area clear, but it was decided that it would be too expensive to do so. When laying foundations for the new building workmen found an old well that was still full of water, and had been there for hundreds of years underneath the previous building. (*M. Sale*)

The Three Pigeons on the Wendover Road. This was the first pub you came to when entering Aylesbury from the south. It has since been demolished and the site is now occupied by houses. (*M. Sale*)

The Bear in Walton Street. This quaint old pub was set in a row of very old buildings and was particularly small inside. To the rear there was an old forge which is seen on page 111. All these buildings have now gone and there is a roundabout here. (*M. Sale*)

The Forester's Arms in Pebble Lane. This was locally known as the Flea Pit because of its scruffy interior, and also because of the number of odd people that used to frequent the place. Since the pub's closure in the 1970s it has been Pebbles restaurant and is now a fruit and veg shop. (*M. Sale*)

A quiet view of Kingsbury, probably photographed on a Sunday. Here we see, on the left, the Red Lion Inn which is said to be a fifteenth-century building. In the distance just below the church is The Rockwood, which is another very old building. The modern building in between the two pubs was occupied by Aylesbury Record Centre on the ground floor. The Record Centre was a popular place in the 1960s. Both of the pubs have since had their names changed. The Red Lion is now the Hobgoblin and The Rockwood has become the Lobster Pot. (*M. Sale*)

Now let us take a look inside one of the pubs. This is the interior of the Eagle in Kingsbury in 1967. The photograph was taken during the promotion for the film of the World Cup of 1966. It was loaned to me by Liz Atkinson (then Langford), who is seen here wearing the Odeon cinema hat. She is standing next to Steve and Sally, the then landlord and landlady. The Eagle was quite a small pub and was also very narrow. It closed in 1975, but the building is still there today and has retained its large iron sign bracket. (*L. Atkinson*)

The Bell Hotel in Market Square. A lot of alterations have been made to this place over the years. When you go inside you find that it is a timber-framed building, which indicates its age. In the early 1920s an extra floor was added and the exterior was remodelled, including the addition of a bay window facing the Market Square. Today the hotel remains largely unchanged in appearance from when this photograph was taken. (*M. Sale*)

The Six Grapes at the bottom of Market Square. The entrance to this pub was at the side, while at the front was the wine merchant James Pettit & Co., which was established in 1737. This view shows the old building at the rear before it was altered and extended in 1967 to become the pub we know today. (*M. Sale*)

The Greyhound in Churchill Avenue, Southcourt. The licence for this pub was moved to these new premises because of the demolition of the original building at the bottom of Silver Street. The new pub opened in April 1957 and was the first to be built on the Southcourt estate. (*M. Sale*)

The Steeplechase, Taylor Road. This was the second pub to be built in Southcourt and the licence was transferred from the old Falcon which stood in Great Western Street. While it was being constructed, there was a competition held to find a name. For a while it was to be called the Churchill Arms, but apparently Winston Churchill heard of this and decided he didn't like the idea of a pub being named after him. After a rethink the current title was chosen to commemorate the fact that the pub stood on the site of the old Aylesbury racecourse. It was opened in June 1957. (*M. Sale*)

The Buckingham Arms, Buckingham Street. This pub has changed very little over the years but it has not always been known as the Buckingham Arms. In the early nineteenth century the pub was listed in directories as the Black Boy. The pub is still there and has recently been painted a rather stark turquoise blue. Some people have unusual taste. (*R.W. Powell*)

The Queen's Head in Temple Square, seen here from Temple Street. In its quiet setting, this place has hardly changed over the years. During all the development in the 1960s it was decided to preserve this part of town because these buildings were apparently in better condition than the ones pulled down in the development zone. (*M. Sale*)

The sign of the Nag's Head in Cambridge Street. This pub stood here until the early 1990s when it was demolished with its adjacent buildings to make way for a new road called Upper Hundreds Way. The large building in the background is St John's Church, which has also disappeared. (*M. Sale*)

The Chandos Hotel, High Street. Seen here caught by the sun, this Victorian hotel and adjacent buildings in Exchange Street were demolished in about 1981 to make way for a large office block called 66 The Exchange. (*M. Sale*)

The two pubs at the bottom right-hand side of Market Square. On the left is the small pub called the Cross Keys and next door on the right is the Coach & Horses. All of these buildings had to go in the redevelopment, and are seen again on page 81. (*M. Sale*)

The Bull's Head Hotel, Market Square. This is how it looked after the demolition of the buildings in front, which were occupied by estate agent Percy Black & Co and the chemist T.M. Ashford, who by this time had moved to the other side of the square. In a similar situation to that of the King's Head, consideration was given to the idea of leaving the hotel exposed (*see* page 33). But it was decided that this would cost too much, and so the area was built up again. (*M. Sale*)

The White Hart in Exchange Street. The pub was moved to this site when the old building in Market Square was demolished in 1864 to make way for the Corn Exchange. The building seen here was altered in later years and by 1983 it had been demolished to make way for a large office block. The statue that stood above the door apparently still exists, but no one is quite sure where. (*M. Sale*)

The Horse & Jockey, Wendover Road. We see it here in pre-gyratory days when its setting was rather more peaceful. To the right of the pub is the entrance to Walton Place. This particular area disappeared in 1969 when the gyratory was built. Today the pub still stands and is known as The Aristocrat. (*M. Sale*)

3

From the Freezing Winter of 1963 to 1964

The frozen canal at High Bridge Walk, 1963. (*M. Sale*)

Princes Road, winter 1963, a winter that will go down in history as one of Britain's coldest. There was snow everywhere for months until March 1963 when it finally began to thaw. (*M. Sale*)

The canal frozen over just down from Highbridge Walk. At this time the ice was inches thick and you could easily cycle along it. It seems a strange sight as we just don't get a lot of snow in Aylesbury any more. (*M. Sale*)

Another view of the canal, this time at the basin end. Only at the weir has the ice been broken, and judging by the footprints and the long curving mark on the snow, some children have been pulling a sled along the surface of the canal. (*M. Sale*)

Now this is what you call an icicle! The photograph was taken in Silver Street at the rear of ladies' outfitters Duckworth & Cooper, who were in Market Square. It was so cold that temperatures were reputed to be as low as -30°C. Conditions caused absolute havoc for vehicles everywhere. (*M. Sale*)

Friarage Passage looking towards town, May 1963. The photograph was taken from near the railway station, and the large building right of centre is the rear of Bucks Motor Co. in Great Western Street. All that remains today of this path is the short section between the new Friarage Road and Bourbon Street, but the two tall trees on the extreme left now overlook the car park of Safeway supermarket. (*R.W. Powell*)

Cambridge Street, 1963. This view shows the row of houses between Upper Hundreds and St John's Street. A couple of years later they were all demolished as they were 'unfit for human habitation'. In the 1950s and '60s Aylesbury saw many of these smaller dwellings disappear. Note the awful state of Saunders' greengrocer's shop on the right: to say it was badly neglected is a bit of an understatement. (*M. Sale*)

Walton Street, summer 1963. This is one of Aylesbury's most handsome buildings just before demolition: Walton Cottage (an unusual name given the size of the building) stood opposite the old county offices. To the rear were extensive gardens stretching as far as the railway line; they included some old timber-framed buildings that adjoined the main structure. The demolition of fine architecture like this is pure vandalism. (*M. Sale*)

A little further up Walton Street was a row of buildings that included Lucas's House Furnishers on the right, and on the left is E. Paragreen, leather merchants. This was the first business to be sacrificed in the development and was demolished in August 1963. (*M. Sale*)

The aftermath of the fire at Hazell Watson & Viney's paper warehouse Saturday 28 September 1963. The fire started the night before, and as it burned through the night there were concerns that the adjacent houses in Victoria Street might go up too. Many of them had to be evacuated, and the occupants had to stay in friends' and neighbours' houses for the night. (*F. Fountain*)

This is how the warehouse looked before the fire. It took a long time to get it under control and it wasn't until daybreak that it was finally put out. Hazell's stated that it lost about 4.5 million books in the big fire. That's a lot of paper. (*F. Fountain*)

This bit of Aylesbury was often called the Kingsbury bottleneck, and is seen here in 1963. It seems to have been a busy day at the Bonnet Box, which sold hats, and ladies' and children's clothing. The rather forlorn building next door was Crouch's the jewellers, which was empty and awaiting demolition. (*M. Sale*)

Looking towards Kingsbury, 1963. Taken on the same wet day as the picture above, this view shows the original site of the Bacon Shop. At this time there were two shops, the other being in Cambridge Street; since the buildings seen here were demolished, the Cambridge Street store is now the only one left. The building on the left is Lucas's corner shop. (*M. Sale*)

The High Street, early 1964. In the centre are the premises of home removals firm and furnishers V. Robinson & Sons. There are two shops shown here; the one on the left sold furniture and the one to the right is the china department. The first shop to the left of Robinson's is ironmonger J.H. Bradford and further down the street on the right is the china shop Clarke's. The last shop on the right is the gentlemen's outfitter George Tough. The block occupied by Robinson's and Clarke's has since been rebuilt, and is now the food store Iceland. (*M. Sale*)

Two Victorian buildings at the very top of Buckingham Road, 1964. On the left is the Primitive Methodist chapel, which stood on the corner of New Street. It was demolished in about 1967 for road widening. The other building seen here is Melrose House, which was a doctor's surgery. This building was demolished in the early 1970s, but the brick and stone wall remained for many years until after the mid-1990s, when this whole corner was taken back to allow for more road widening. (*M. Sale*)

Earlier in this book we saw various pubs around the town in the 1960s. Here is a pub that stood in Station Street – the Railway Tavern. This replaced a Victorian building in about 1910 and was demolished in the late 1960s. To the right of this building was the site of Aylesbury's first railway station. (*R.W. Powell*)

Activity in the High Street as Jarvis's clothing store has a new extension built, early 1964. This was the second phase of expansion, which was planned to include all of the buildings between the bank, on the right, and the Round House at the end. It's a good job that the rest never got built because the proposed massive building would have completely overshadowed everything around it. (*M. Sale*)

Cambridge Street, 1964. This view has not changed much, although the direction of traffic on this part of the street has been reversed. Note the bin attached to the lamp-post in the foreground: it says 'Aylesbury's Best Value – Blackboy Supermarket – Why Pay More?' The supermarket opened in 1959 and was situated in Buckingham Street next to the Methodist church. (*M. Sale*)

Buckingham Street in 1964. Another view that has changed very little. The white building on the far left was part of Chamberlin's motor engineers. The site is now Sainsbury's. The turning just behind the lamp-post was the entrance to Percy Black's auction rooms. The passage still exists today and leads to an office block. (*M. Sale*)

Silver Street, 1964. This view shows the rear of the buildings that fronted Market Square and illustrates just how steep the street was. The Cross Keys pub can be seen on the right and next to it further up the street is the Coach & Horses. Note the different positions of windows on the Cross Keys. (*M. Sale*)

Castle Street, 1964. This view seems unchanged since this photograph was taken, but the cottage on the right behind the telephone pole has been demolished. On the opposite side of the road, where the fence is, the Plume of Feathers pub once stood. The white cottage on the left was another of Castle Street's old pubs, The Half Moon, which closed long before this photograph was taken. The building is still called The Old Half Moon. (*M. Sale*)

Hale Leys Square on a warm summer's day, 1964. The jumble of buildings to the right is the rear of the Bull's Head Hotel, which fronted Market Square. The tall Victorian building opposite is the Westminster Bank, which has since been rebuilt and is now the NatWest Bank. The road seen here led from Market Square to the hotel garage and car park. (*M. Sale*)

Another Hale Leys Square scene, 1964. To the left is the old timber-framed building that was Hunt's, which sold typewriters and other office equipment. The main entrance was round in Market Square. Veronique next door sold ladies' fashion and was in part of the same building as the Westminster Bank. Everything in Hale Leys Square has gone, and it is now a shopping centre which takes its name from this area. (*M. Sale*)

Looking down Coopers Yard, 1964. This lane runs off Buckingham Street and ends at the rear of New Street. At the end of the lane the back of some houses in the latter street can be seen. The old white-painted buildings on the left are part of Harper's mason's yard, which have now completely gone, as has everything else in this photograph. (*M. Sale*)

The cattle market area, 1964. Here we see the premises of T. Loader, the corn merchants who occupied the old Corn Exchange buildings. They also had a shop in Kingsbury that supplied all sorts of things for pet owners and gardeners. The painted building seen here was demolished later to make way for the Civic Centre. Just beyond it is the rear of the County Hall. (*M. Sale*)

Another view of the old Corn Exchange building, 1964. The tall building in the centre is the rear of the Town Hall. At the top of the alley is the Six Grapes pub with the large roof of the Borough Assembly Hall stretching across behind. The Civic Centre now occupies the site of the old Corn Exchange buildings. (*M. Sale*)

If you were to turn and face the other way from the view in the picture above, this is what you would have seen in 1964 – looking down through the cattle market towards Exchange Street, with Richards timber yard facing you. This picture was obviously taken on a quiet day. Normally the cattle market would have been alive with the sights (and smells!) of various animals. Now all this has vanished, and the site is occupied by the recently built multi-screen cinema. (*M. Sale*)

A fine view of Parson's Fee, 1964. This is one of Aylesbury's oldest thoroughfares and thankfully it survives. This photograph was taken before the cobbles were relaid: there is quite a ridge in the middle of the road, caused by years of cars and horse-drawn carriages trundling up and down. The entrance under the large tree is that of Prebendal House. (*M. Sale*)

Mill Way, 1964. This view is looking towards town, and St Mary's Church can be seen on the left above the houses. Mill Way no longer leads to the mill as it was demolished a few years ago. On its site there is now housing. To the right behind the gate is the playground of St Mary's School. These school buildings may also disappear soon as St Mary's has recently moved to the new Fairford Leys estate. (*M. Sale*)

The top of Silver Street, 1964. This view illustrates just how narrow it was at this end. To the left is Market Street while on the right is Bourbon Street. The Dark Lantern pub is in the centre, and today it is the only building left in the area that is over 100 years old. (*M. Sale*)

Market Square, 1964, showing the newly extended shoe shop of Freeman Hardy & Willis. The older building was rendered and painted in a rather lacklustre grey, which made it fit in quite well with the coming of Friars Square. For the other buildings, demolition was imminent, as is indicated by the sign of the contractors McAlpine on the Cross Keys pub on the far left. An older scene appears on page 13. (*M. Sale*)

Great Western Street from the bottom of Market Square, 1964. As is seen by the 'Last Day' painted on the side of clothes shop Weaver to Wearer on the far right, demolition was imminent. The buildings stretching down the street still had three years left before they too were demolished. (*M. Sale*)

One of the two lion statues basking in the sun in Market Square. They were presented to the town in 1888 by Baron Ferdinand de Rothschild. The Rothschilds have made their mark on the town over the years with the appearance of various buildings that were commissioned by them – for example, the Public Baths in Bourbon Street, the Victoria Club in Kingsbury and the Literary Institute in Temple Street. (*M. Sale*)

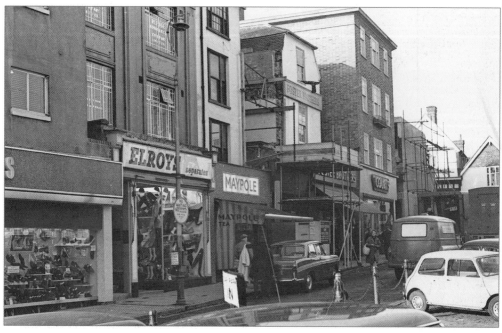

Market Square, 1964. The scaffolding seen here next to Maypole dairy provisions was for the extension of Foster Brothers' gentlemen's outfitter. The building that was demolished was Home & Colonial Stores. Maypole's closed in the latter part of 1964. Further up the square there is more building work going on in front of the King's Head. (*M. Sale*)

A fine summer's day in Market Square, 1964. This is a nice view of the busy market with people mingling around the fruit and flower stalls. The canopy seen top right is that of the shoe shop, Freeman Hardy & Willis. In the distance just beyond the Bell Hotel is the crane which was being used on the building site of the County Offices. (*M. Sale*)

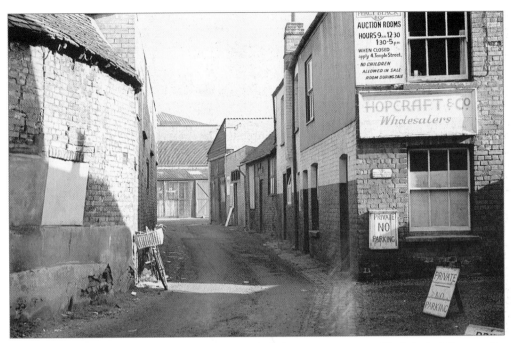

This lane ran off Buckingham Street next to Chamberlin's motor engineers. All of the buildings on the left-hand side and the large one at the end belonged to the firm. Stretching down on the right is Percy Black's auction rooms. Everything seen here has now gone. The buildings on the left have been replaced by Sainsbury's while on the right a car park now serves a large office block at the end. (*M. Sale*)

Some handsome buildings in Walton Street, 1964. These houses were situated between the Aylesbury Brewery Company and Walton Parish Hall. Apart from the two buildings on the far right, these would all be gone in a couple of years together with the brewery buildings, to be replaced with Planar House (page 114). (*R.W. Powell*)

Looking up Friarage Road, 1964. This is a good view of the old slaughterhouse. Note the various different doors and little windows, quite unlike the more formal buildings in Bourbon Street, which can be seen at the top of the road. (*M. Sale*)

Silver Lane, 1964. This narrow lane ran parallel with Bourbon Street and went from the old Friarage Road through to Silver Street at the other end. The white buildings on the right were part of the old slaughterhouse seen in the previous photograph. (*M. Sale*)

Another view of Friarage Road, 1964. This road ran from Bourbon Street to Great Western Street, which is seen at the end. The fenced-off ground to the right was once the site of a pub called the Square & Compasses, which was demolished in 1962. The nearest building, with the gable-end window, was the premises of tent maker J. Marks, with the Friarage Motor Cycle Company next door. (*M. Sale*)

The rear of Great Western Street, 1964. The lane pictured here ran off Great Western Street and met Friarage Road, in the centre. The area to the right was a triangle of land that was full of buildings until 1959, when they were demolished. The cleared area was then used as a temporary car park. (*M. Sale*)

The passage that went under the Old Beams Restaurant in Market Square, 1964. The name of the restaurant was appropriate as it was a very old timber-framed building. The end of the passage came out just opposite Jones & Cocks's former premises, now part of The Lantern pub. Today there is only one passage left: that is Stockwell Passage, which is at right angles to this one and comes out on Market Square. (*M. Sale*)

Looking along Temple Street towards Bourbon Street, 1964. This picture shows the handsome building that was home to grocer and wine merchant M.T. Cocks & Co. The large lettering on the building had remained the same since the 1930s. Just to the left of the building is the narrow entrance to Silver Street. In Temple Street on the right are the new premises of estate agents Percy Black & Co., which had recently moved from Market Square when its original building was demolished. (*R.W. Powell*)

Friarage Passage, 1964: the rear of houses that were in Friarage Road. The large building on the right was the former Methodist chapel, which at this time was used by the Ex-Services Club, and also by the Mary Lord School of Dancing. (*M. Sale*)

The bottom end of Great Western Street, 1964. The *Bucks Herald* had its office here before it moved to its present site in Exchange Street. To the rear through the gates was the place you could go in and buy newspapers. Up the street in the distance is the sign of the Railway Hotel. (*M. Sale*)

Parson's Fee, 1964. Were it not for the cars in this photograph it could have been taken much more recently: today it still looks very much the same. The house seen here is St Osyth's, which in days gone by was a farmhouse. (*M. Sale*)

Dark Lantern Passage, 1964. In this area are the only existing medieval alleyways in Aylesbury. The building on the right with the rather cluttered shop window was the premises of Home & Hardware Stores. At the end of the alley is the very narrow part of the top of Silver Street. The old timber-framed building was at the rear of M.T. Cocks, grocer and wine merchant, the front of which is seen at the bottom of page 64. (*M. Sale*)

Great Western Street, 1964. The Bucks Motor Company sold Wolseley, Riley and Morris motor cars among other marques. As with many other businesses of the time, they were forced to close because of the redevelopment of the area. (*M. Sale*)

Looking down Great Western Street, 1964. We are standing by the petrol pumps at the Bucks Motor Company, which is seen above. The curving line of cobbles marks how narrow the road was before widening took place; there used to be a row of large Victorian houses along here. At the bottom of the street past the *Bucks Herald* office is the railway station. (*M. Sale*)

Looking down the side of the Railway Hotel in Great Western Street to a row of Victorian houses in Friarage Terrace. Rising above them in the distance is the crane which was being used in the construction of the new county offices and library. (*M. Sale*)

Walton Street, 1964. The site of the car showroom of Claude Rye was originally occupied by Eborn's garage, which was sold to Rye in 1960. As is seen on the sign, the firm sold motorcycles and that unforgettable 1960s fad, the bubble car. (*M. Sale*)

4

Demolition Under Way, 1964–65

A timber-strewn view of Silver Street being demolished, late 1964.
(*M. Sale*)

Before we take a look at the destruction of the Silver Street area let us see what was on the outskirts of the town. This photograph and the next show the site of Bedgrove in 1964 before it was developed. Like many of the estates around the town, this was once a farm. The main farm buildings are seen through the trees on the left. Today this has completely gone and is covered by Pevensey Close and Ambleside. The square hole in the foreground was dug as part of an archaeological survey, which is explained in more detail in the next caption. (*M. Sale*)

Turning to the right a little we can see houses in Craigwell Avenue and Limes Avenue in the distance. This field was at first believed to be the site of the lost medieval village of Caldecote. After a few years of study it was decided that it was in fact the site of Bedgrove itself. Archaeologists digging the site between 1964 and 1966 found the remains of the houses that used to stand here, together with nearly 4,000 sherds of pottery. This whole site has been completely covered by the Jansel Square shopping centre. When a place has changed so much it is hard to imagine it as it was. (*M. Sale*)

A look down Silver Street, 1964. Work has begun on the destruction of this old street, and piles of timber lie strewn everywhere. Some of this timber was salvaged while the rest was burnt. The building on the immediate left with the rather quaint street lamp is Jones & Cocks, ironmongers, one of only two buildings to remain in Silver Street, the other being the Dark Lantern pub. (*M. Sale*)

A worker stands and watches his colleague rooting around in the roof of a building in Silver Street. A cloud of dust appears from the discarded bits of wood. It must be noted that no scaffolding or safety hats were being used: it was a dangerous business. (*M. Sale*)

Another Silver Street scene. A workman's jacket rests on an old armchair in among the strewn timber. Some of the trees that were used for these beams were likely to have been felled some 400 or 500 years ago. (*M. Sale*)

Another view of the familiar buildings in Silver Street. It is ironic that quite a lot was learnt about the age of these buildings by demolishing them. It is a shame they had to go at all. A man is standing on the far left of the photograph looking at the destruction before him: it seems he can't believe what he's seeing. He probably thought he would never see old Aylesbury disappear like this. (*M. Sale*)

Looking towards Bourbon Street from the old Friarage Road. The half-demolished building in the foreground is the old slaughterhouse which is seen on page 62. On the left by the van is the entrance to Silver Lane. (*M. Sale*)

Looking down a derelict Silver Lane from Friarage Road. At the end of the lane, a workman is climbing up a ladder to strip the roof of a timber-framed building. The half-demolished building nearest is the previously mentioned slaughterhouse. (*M. Sale*)

Friarage Road, with another view of the old slaughterhouse. Beyond the old buildings, the top of the County Hall can be seen. The Victorian building on the right with a central door was used by butcher George Rayner. One of his shops was in Great Western Street – just a few yards from here. (*M. Sale*)

A similar view to the previous picture but this time taken from further away and showing the temporary car park that was used after the Public Baths were demolished. It must be pointed out that at the time there were not many official car parks, so any spare piece of ground was readily turned into a makeshift parking area. (*M. Sale*)

A workman walks along a rather forlorn Silver Lane. Note the temporary path that has been made through the rubble. In the background are buildings in Friarage Road, and beyond them is the Ex-Services Club in Friarage Passage. (*M. Sale*)

Looking down Silver Lane again but this time from the Friarage Road end. Another old armchair is discarded among the rubble, probably thrown out of one of the buildings along here. (*M. Sale*)

This time we look down Silver Lane from the Jones & Cocks end. Their building is seen on the right with a bicycle leaning against the wall. The large building on the right was the rear of Old Beams Restaurant, which was tucked away in Market Square. (*M. Sale*)

A little later on in 1964 and the southern side of Silver Street was almost completely gone. The supporting brick wall that was put there a couple of years before was now the only thing left standing. I wonder what the two old men seen here are talking about as they look upon this depressing sight. (*M. Sale*)

This photograph is to the immediate left of the one above and looks down Great Western Street. It is the area where the two pubs of the Falcon and the Greyhound once stood. To the left is the temporary car park that was formed after the demolition of buildings on that site. Note the man stripping the roof of the building in the centre of picture. (*M. Sale*)

This view shows buildings on the southern side of Bourbon Street being demolished. The one being bulldozed here had been the offices of the *Bucks Advertiser*. Through the clouds of dust in the distance the familiar roof lines of the Town Hall and County Hall can be seen. (*M. Sale*)

Another Bourbon Street scene, showing the now demolished premises of M.T. Cocks, wine merchants. In the new development, this particular area became the widened entrance to the remaining part of Silver Street. The ancient building occupied by Home & Hardware Stores seen here was also demolished a few years later (*see* page 118). (*M. Sale*)

A view of the Market Square through the rubble-strewn Silver Street area. This photograph was taken from Friarage Road, and shows in the foreground the timber uprights that were part of the old slaughterhouse. (*M. Sale*)

Another view of Market Square this time from Great Western Street. In the distance, just to the left of the Clock Tower, a new building is going up on the site of T.M. Ashford's and Percy Black & Co's old premises. On the left is Friarage Road. (*M. Sale*)

Market Square, 1964. This shot shows just how old some of the buildings were in the Silver Street area. The exposed roof timbers seen here indicate that this particular building was probably fifteenth or sixteenth century in date but had been refronted. This part of Market Square was to become the main entrance of Friars Square. (*M. Sale*)

Looking a bit further down Market Square, 1964. This is the last building standing at that end of Silver Street. It is amazing that there were no screens around the site to protect the public from falling masonry. The rules for health and safety were different then. (*M. Sale*)

Another view of Market Square. This shows, to the centre and right of the picture, the remains of the Coach & Horses and Cross Keys pubs. What a sad sight this is – it looks like a wartime scene. Although Aylesbury hardly had any bomb damage during the Second World War, the town planners certainly made up for it in the 1960s. (*M. Sale*)

Exactly the same view as above but a few days later. The pubs and their adjacent buildings have gone now, and you can see Bourbon Street in the distance. Notice the temporary barrier that has been put up to stop people falling down into what were the cellars of the demolished buildings. These were all filled in later on. (*M. Sale*)

Back in Great Western Street, the Bucks Motor Company building is being made ready for demolition. All of the windows and doors have been removed, and some are leaning up against a wall inside. (*M. Sale*)

The clearance is almost complete now, with just one building left to go: the old Beams Restaurant is the narrow white building just left of centre. In 1964 you could briefly see far and wide across the town centre. This view shows the natural gradient of this area, which was soon to be dug away. (*M. Sale*)

A view of the new County Offices being built in about April 1965. As can be seen, the construction of this unusual building is progressing well. Some local people call it 'Pooley's Folly', after its architect, Fred Pooley. The new street in the foreground is part of the new Friarage Road, which later in 1965 ploughed on through these Victorian buildings. On the left is the Railway Hotel. (*M. Sale*)

It's May 1965 and preparation work has started on the foundations of Friars Square. Already deep excavation is being carried out by the tall drilling machine seen here. All that is left of the demolished buildings is a few bricks here and there, pressed into the soil by the site's heavy vehicles. (*M. Sale*)

Another view of the Friars Square site taken at the same time as the previous photograph. In the foreground about 10 ft or so of soil has been dug away to make the area more level. This was in preparation for the underground market that was to be constructed here. After the revamp of Friars Square in 1993, the Cloisters shopping area replaced the market. (*M. Sale*)

Looking further down towards the railway station. The buildings to the left are in Great Western Street. This photograph was probably taken from Bourbon Street, which would have been a good vantage point over the site. In the foreground the excavation must be particularly deep, as it has had to be shored up to stop it collapsing. (*M. Sale*)

A view down Oxford Road, May 1965. On the left are the remains of the Rising Sun pub, which was being demolished in preparation for the new dual carriageway, Friarage Road. The large tree and everything on the left-hand side of the road were soon gone too. This view shows well how narrow the old road was. All the buildings on the right survive today. (*M. Sale*)

Looking in the opposite direction along Oxford Road towards the Hen & Chickens pub. Demolition has begun on the row of buildings that were between Castle Street and White Hill: they all had to come down because Friarage Road came through here. Note the man on the roof of the tall buildings of Oxford Road Stores: you wouldn't catch me up there! On the left is the wall of St Mary's School. (*M. Sale*)

The entrance to Ludds Alley, which went behind these cottages in Oxford Road and came out on to White Hill. These buildings are awaiting demolition, and in a couple of weeks they were gone. The house on the right was once a pub called the Eight Bells. Careful inspection of the brickwork to the left of the removed window shows a T-shaped marking where the old sign was affixed. (*M. Sale*)

A derelict house in Ludds Alley, May 1965. Aylesbury once had many of these narrow little alleyways dotted around the town. This particular one was probably about 300 years old. Ludds Alley was swept away completely, and the site is now occupied by the car park of Big Hand Mo's pub. (*M. Sale*)

Oxford Road, looking towards the entrance to Castle Street. Below the large tree in the middle distance are the remains of the Rising Sun. On the right are the gardens of the row of houses that still remain today. That side of the road was untouched by development. The pavement on the opposite side of the road is now the central reservation of the dual carriageway of Friarage Road. (*M. Sale*)

The temporary bar that was used when the Hen & Chickens was closed for demolition. Just beyond it are houses in White Hill – another road that has been straightened and widened. The empty Hen & Chickens pub can just be seen on the right. (*M. Sale*)

Now we come to a lovely part of town – St Mary's Square. Thankfully this area has changed very little and is a tranquil setting compared with all the noisy traffic that is just a few hundred yards away. The hanging sign seen here is that of the Derby Arms pub, which is shown on page 23. (*M. Sale*)

How to spoil a perfectly good view. The canal is another pleasant part of Aylesbury, and this concrete edifice growing on the horizon just ruins the scenery. There is one good thing about the County Offices though, and that is the view you get from them It is good to see that the boat yard is still a busy place today, and is always packed with lots of barges. (*M. Sale*)

Walton Street looking towards town, October 1965. This is a nice view of the row of buildings that was later replaced by a roundabout. Immediately on the right is a small café called the Copper Kettle. In the centre is the Bear Inn. Just beyond these buildings are the old County Offices and the former police station, which are still there today. (*M. Sale*)

Looking further up Walton Street, this photograph was taken at the same time as the one above. As can be seen by the large cranes in the distance, the foundations of Friars Square were being laid. Just beyond the cranes are houses in Bourbon Street. The large white building on the left is the Old House which is facing Exchange Street where a lorry is waiting to pull out. The Old House has since been demolished. (*M. Sale*)

A view along the canal towards town, May 1965. In the distance the half-built County Offices can be seen and just to the left is Nestlé's chimney. This same view cannot be seen very clearly today because there are lots of trees along the towpath. The opposite side of the canal is now occupied by industrial units. (*M. Sale*)

A town horizon seen from Cambridge Street, October 1965. Clearly visible are the County Offices, now nearing completion. Attached to the left-hand side of the building is the temporary external lift that was used to deliver workmen up and down the various floors. quite a frightening journey if you were afraid of heights! On page 46 there is a view of Cambridge Street but looking in the opposite direction; it shows the row of houses that were in the fenced-off area. (*M. Sale*)

A view along New Street, 1965. Celebrating sixty years of Singer cars is Lawrence's garage on the right. Behind the houses further down the street the telephone exchange can be seen. These days New Street is much wider and has lost all of the buildings on the right-hand side of the road: it is now very busy. (*M. Sale*)

Kingsbury, 1965. The original bus station with a large bus shelter is in the centre. Beyond is the familiar line of buildings that has remained largely unchanged since this picture was taken, apart from the buildings to the right (then home of Aylesbury Motor Company) which have been rebuilt. (*M. Sale*)

A fine view of Kingsbury showing Ivatt's shoe shop, October 1965. This is an interesting view as it shows the small Victorian shopfront to the left together with its more modern counterpart. Another peculiar feature of the picture is that the external appearance of Adams' is missing something. It is the familiar black lettering 'Tobacco & Cigars 31' that the building is known for. This did reappear later. More recently the front has been re-rendered and the letters have been painted on again, although they look a bit different to the originals. (*M. Sale*)

Looking towards Buckingham Street from Kingsbury. The people in the centre of picture are looking down a gaping hole, which is possibly the remains of the cellar of the building that used to be there. All that remains to be done is to fill it in and take up the old pathway, in order to make the turning much easier for traffic. In the background to the left is the well-known baker, Page's of Aylesbury, which closed in the 1980s. (*M. Sale*)

Cambridge Street, October 1965. This picture shows the temporary shops that were built to accommodate some of the Silver Street area businesses while Friars Square was constructed. To the right, beyond the gleaming Morris Oxford, the protruding sign of the Nags Head can be seen. Opposite is the Oddfellows' Arms, with St John's Church standing proudly behind it. (*M. Sale*)

Buckingham Street, October 1965. After the old slaughterhouse was demolished, its site was used as a car park. The building in the foreground is Baker's cycle and toy shop. The window display advertises the fireworks being sold inside: Baker's always had a good selection. The shop has since closed. (*M. Sale*)

Looking down a newly widened White Hill, October 1965. To the left are cars parked in Whitehall Street, which by this time had lost all of its buildings on the north side to accommodate this dual carriageway. At the bottom of the hill is the newly built roundabout. In recent years it has been turned into a multi-roundabout system, which seems to do little to alleviate the traffic flow problems through this part of town. (*M. Sale*)

The construction of the second carriageway of Friarage Road in progress, October 1965. Both of these new bits of road went straight through the garden of Friarscroft, which is the large Victorian building on the left. Also on the left, the turning for Rickfords Hill is being widened. (*M. Sale*)

Oxford Road, October 1965. This is an unusual view showing the site of the Rising Sun, which is indicated by the pub's sign holder. This photograph also clearly illustrates just how much soil had to be carted away to make the second carriageway of the new Friarage Road. (*M. Sale*)

Men at work on the Friars Square site, October 1965. This photograph was taken from Bourbon Street looking towards the Bell Hotel in Market Square. There were just a few months to go before things started to take shape and this wide open view disappeared forever. (*M. Sale*)

Buckingham Street, October 1965. This picture shows the first Tesco supermarket in the town. Formerly occupied by the Blackboy Supermarket, this building was taken over by Tesco in July 1965. The company remained there until March 1967 when it moved into Friars Square. Today this part of the street looks much the same, as all of these buildings are still here. (*M. Sale*)

A view up the High Street taken at the same time as the previous photograph. Judging by what the people are wearing it was quite a chilly day. In the centre is Robinson's furnishings and removals with Clarke's china shop next to it. To the left of Robinson's is Home & Hardware Stores; the latter was a newcomer to the High Street having just moved into the former premises of Bradford's ironmongers. This was probably because the future of the firm's main shop in Market Street was unsure – questions were being asked about its safety. It is seen on page 118. (*M. Sale*)

5

From 1966 to the End of the Decade

A view of Great Western Street from the railway footbridge, 1966. (*M. Sale*)

Exchange Street at the junction with High Street, January 1966. This photograph shows just how narrow the road used to be: it only took a few steps to cross it. All of the buildings on the left would soon be gone to allow for road widening. The building on the right is the Chandos Hotel, which has also disappeared. (*M. Sale*)

Now we are right down by the railway station in Great Western Street. Franklins Fuels was situated next to the *Bucks Herald* office, which just to the left. When phase two of Friars Square was completed, Franklins Fuels moved into a unit that was built on the site of the Railway Hotel. (*M. Sale*)

Walton Street, summer 1966. Walton Baptist chapel is being demolished. Originally there was a burial ground in front of the chapel and when the street was widened for the first time in the late 1950s the burials had to be moved. Next to it is the original site of the Elmhurst Youth Centre: it moved to its present site in Fairfax Crescent in 1969. (*M. Sale*)

The derelict Brook House Hotel was situated just next to the railway bridge on Oxford Road. Behind is the large gasometer in Gatehouse Road, which by this time was the main site of the gas works. The old site behind Railway Street was disused at the time. On the site today is an office which also uses the name Brook House. (*M. Sale*)

One of Jarvis's shopfronts in the High Street during the Borough of Aylesbury Jubilee celebrations, 25 June to 2 July 1966. Lots of shops had displays commemorating this event. Jarvis's came up with this one, which compared the fashions of 1916 with those of 1966. (*M. Sale*)

Another store celebrating the jubilee was Weatherhead's bookshop in Kingsbury. Its display compared the developments in printing technology over the previous fifty years. This shop was a favourite for book lovers for many years and had a good secondhand section at the back. It closed in about 1989 after being Dillons and then Bargain Books for a short time and then the Emporium tea rooms. Now the building is occupied by Pizza Express. (*M. Sale*)

The jubilee celebrations kicked off with a cycle race, which started in the Market Square. Here the riders are going through Kingsbury. The course consisted of five laps through Whitchurch, Oving, Waddesdon crossroads and back to Aylesbury, covering 68 miles in total. As can be seen the weather conditions were not perfect – every rider and indeed most of the spectators getting a good soaking. The winner was a Bletchley rider, Dick Goodman, who collected prize money of £20. (*M. Sale*)

The celebrations ended on Saturday 2 July 1966 with a carnival procession. It started in Gatehouse Road and then went up White Hill, down Buckingham Street, through Market Square and down the High Street. Here we see nineteen-year-old Jubilee Queen Christine Hall on her float, going past the Congregational church in the High Street. (*M. Sale*)

Another view of the carnival procession through the High Street. There was a good turn out on the day and the weather was fine. In the evening a fiesta was held in the Market Square which was attended by thousands of people. It was penned the 'Hobble on the Cobbles'. There was music and dancing and of course lots of drink, and it lasted until midnight. The police were in attendance, but apparently they didn't make a single arrest. (*M. Sale*)

This yard was opposite the Bell Hotel in Walton Street and was used for customer parking. Also parked here is the van belonging to Tilbury's, the butchers, who at the time had a shop in Walton Street. The light-coloured building behind the van is the rear of Samuel's shop, which stood on the corner of Great Western Street and Walton Street. (*M. Sale*)

A delightful view of a pair of cottages that stood in Green End, just off Rickfords Hill. Originally these were in an area that was full of old buildings, but over the years all were gradually demolished leaving these cottages standing virtually alone. In recent years they too have been demolished and replaced with new houses, which ironically are described as being in a conservation area. (*M. Sale*)

Looking up Great Western Street, 1966. As is seen by the scaffolding on the left, phase one of Friars Square was progressing. After a couple more years the whole street had been redeveloped. The Railway Hotel, with its familiar gargoyles, stands on the right. At the top of the street the County Hall and Bell Hotel can be seen. (*M. Sale*)

Great Western Street, from the Market Square end looking towards the railway station, 1966. Tomkins the hairdresser was home to quite a character, seventy-four-year-old Mr Westley, who was known to be a regular in the Falcon and Greyhound pubs. If anyone had their hair cut by him and needed a shave, it was quite a worrying experience as he had rather shaky hands! (*M. Sale*)

This Aylesbury alleyway was situated between two rows of houses in Friarage Terrace, which was off Great Western Street. If you were to walk along this passage you would have come out on Walton Street, just opposite the Bell Hotel. (*M. Sale*)

An immaculate scene in Vale Park, August 1966. The drinking fountain just left of centre stood in Kingsbury from 1914 to 1929. On the left are the tall poplar trees which lined the park along Lovers Walk until recently when they were all chopped down. Today the park is shrinking, as a new swimming pool is being built on the Park Street side. (*M. Sale*)

The flour mill of Hills and Partridge, August 1966. This local firm was based at Walton Mills, where we see a new extension being built. They served the town well over the years, providing bakeries with various types of their high-class flour. The firm closed in the 1990s and most of these buildings have since been demolished. All that remains are the older buildings, which are looking rather neglected. (*M. Sale*)

Looking up Park Street from the entrance to Lovers Walk, August 1966. The level-crossing that is indicated had actually gone by this time: the footbridge and gates had been taken down and the rails dismantled. The buildings nearest along the left-hand side were part of the council's yard. (*M. Sale*)

A wet and windy market day, January 1967. The flower stalls are still up and running at today's market. Beyond the stalls the grey mass of Friars Square can be seen. (*M. Sale*)

Our first view of Friars Square, February 1967. By this time it was partially open and was already home to Cyril Lord Carpets and Currys, with other shops like Tesco, Lucas's furniture store and Boots due to open in March. On the right is the Bourbon Street entrance, while the new sunken open market area is on the left. The open-air and underground markets both opened on 15 March 1967. (*M. Sale*)

Looking along Exchange Street on a beautifully sunny day in about February 1967. This is the entrance to Highbridge Walk. The row of buildings would soon be gone to make way for the widening of Exchange Street. It is hard to see whether this photograph was taken on a warm or a cold day, as the boy running along with the man is wearing a coat and a bobble-hat, while further along the road is a boy in a white shirt and shorts! (*M. Sale*)

Looking along Croft Passage, 1967. This ran from Holy Trinity Church in Walton Street and came out on Highbridge Road. The church can just be seen below the large tree in the centre. On the left is the headquarters of the County Library, while on the right are the huts that were part of the Technical College. These days the passage has largely gone and has been replaced by Croft Road. (*M. Sale*)

Great Western Street, in about April 1967. Demolition has begun in preparation for phase two of Friars Square, which would soon be home to the new bus station and Woolworth's new three-floor store. A great sense of loss is felt when you stand in the tunnel that is here now. (*M. Sale*)

An unusual view of the new County Offices seen from a half-demolished building in Great Western Street, 1967. These days a member of the public would be hard pushed to take a photograph like this in among demolition work. Today building sites are heavily fenced off, and it's difficult to see what's going on. (*M. Sale*)

Friarage Road, 1967. Here we see the last view of the Railway Hotel still standing. The gargoyles have gone off the roof (they are now in the museum) and the adjacent buildings have been demolished. Nikolaus Pevsner in his book on Buckinghamshire buildings described the hotel as an 'engaging little horror'. Today he would find a much bigger horror in its place. (*M. Sale*)

Looking south-west from the County Offices, spring 1967. The cranes are being used to construct the multi-storey car park next to the railway station. The tower block of Aylesbury College is a couple of fields away. In that same field, stretching into the distance on the left, is the huge grass bank that was put there to take the proposed southern approach road, which was to cross the railway track and join up with Great Western Street. The scheme was later dropped. (*M. Sale*)

Looking north from the County Offices, again in spring 1967. There are a lot of people taking advantage of this rare opportunity to view the town from so high up. Below in the centre is the nearly completed first phase of Friars Square, and the busy Market Square is at the bottom right. (*M. Sale*)

Looking along Exchange Street, 1967. In preparation for the forthcoming road widening, these huge old chestnut trees at the end of the Recreation Ground were being chopped down. As is seen by the slice of trunk next to the bench, these trees were quite thick. On the far right is the familiar building that was then occupied by the Electricity Board. It is now used by Aylesbury Vale District Council's planning department, which is soon to move down the road to 66 The Exchange. (*M. Sale*)

An old timber-framed building that stood at the rear of The Bear public house in Walton Street. It was used as a blacksmith's workshop for many years by Fred Page, who was also the landlord of the pub. This building, together with The Bear, was swept away a few months later to make way for the Walton Street roundabout. Progress! (*M. Sale*)

Throughout this book we've looked at various building exteriors. This time we look at a photograph inside The Bear in Walton Street, 1967. The low ceilings and timber-framing illustrate just how old the building was. Note the moulded beams above the fireplace – probably an expensive feature when the building was constructed. (*M. Sale*)

A view of the County Offices from Friars Square, summer 1967. We've seen various car parks here and there in the town throughout this book. Here we see what seems to be an unofficial pram park in use while the prams' owners do some shopping in nearby Tesco and Boots. (*W.A. Grant*)

The open-air market in Friars Square, summer 1967. The market was held here for about twenty-five years until the early 1990s, when it moved back to Market Square after Friars Square had its facelift. Lucas's new furniture store is seen beyond the market stalls next to Cyril Lord Carpets. Later, when Cyril Lord's closed, Lucas's expanded its premises. Lucas's has since moved to Rabans Lane. (*W.A. Grant*)

Great Western Street under development, summer 1967. After all the buildings had been demolished, construction could begin on the second phase of Friars Square, which included the new bus station and Woolworth's new store. As with the first phase, the building work took about two years to complete. In the distance the new multi-storey car park can be seen. (*W.A. Grant*)

Walton Street from the forecourt of motor engineers Cogger & Hawkins, summer 1967. The newly built Planar House replaced the old brewery buildings. Newtown Garage was the first firm to occupy the building, with the Lotus Garden Restaurant and Aylesbury Wine Shop to follow later. After only about twenty-five years, Planar House was demolished, and in the last couple of years a handsome modern building called Millennium House has been erected on part of the site. (*M. Sale*)

Looking down Exchange Street from the High Street end, 1967. This narrow road had a number of traffic problems. In July 1965 a lorry loaded with timber got jammed against the hotel sign when it was trying to get past another vehicle on the opposite side of the road. (*M. Sale*)

Looking down Station Street, 1967. In this book we have seen various roads that have entirely disappeared from the town; and this particular street has only recently vanished. For many years the bottom half of Station Street has been the site of a multi-storey car park. In 1999 work began to construct a large retail unit over the rest of the street. Before this, only two buildings were still left standing: the last to go was the old church hall on the right. Facing us at the bottom of the street is part of the Star Hotel, which stood in Railway Street. (*M. Sale*)

Another view of Station Street, 1967. This time we are looking towards Britannia Street. Immediately on the right is one of Aylesbury's many vanished pubs, the Railway Tavern, which by this time was closed. The disappearance of this street really marked the end of an era for this part of town. This area had once been densely packed with buildings, many of which were residential. Over the years, though, these buildings gradually disappeared as they became disused. Most of the area has recently been redeveloped. (*M. Sale*)

The old police station garage in Exchange Street, 1967. This building stood directly opposite the former police station at the Walton Street end. Beyond the lamp-post on the right, preparation work has begun on the new road to link Friarage Road with the Walton Street roundabout, soon to be constructed. This end of Exchange Street has changed beyond recognition, and in fact the small bit of road pictured here is the only part of the original street to remain. It is now used as a parking area in front of the old station. (*M. Sale*)

A rare view of Brook Street, 1967. At the end of the road are buildings in Walton Street. The row of houses shown here had the evocative name of Tranquil Terrace. These were originally railway workers' homes. Today this view has completely vanished, and the site is now occupied by the 'Blue Leanie' – the offices of Equitable Life. (*M. Sale*)

Looking towards Whitehall Street from the top of White Hill, 1967. The petrol pump on the far left is in the forecourt of the Aylesbury Motor Company. The large building is in a typical 1950s style, quite similar to the Telephone Exchange in New Street. Litton House is now on the site. The row of Victorian houses with the projecting chimneys has also been demolished, and a car park is now on the site. Just beyond the little Austin A30 car is the entrance to Ripon Street. (*M. Sale*)

The sad destruction of one of Aylesbury's timber-framed buildings, Home & Hardware Stores in Market Street. Like many buildings during the 1960s this had a demolition order placed upon it because it was said to be unsafe. It seems that this happened all too easily in those days: the mere hint of anything structurally awry and the whole building had to come down. (*M. Sale*)

An interesting view of the Dark Lantern pub in Silver Street after the demolition of Home & Hardware Stores. This photograph shows how old the building is. It has been suggested that this pub would originally have fronted Market Square. (*M. Sale*)

The former railway station in the High Street, early 1968. The old station forecourt is in the foreground and the wall is the only surviving part of the main station building. The small building adjoining the wall is the premises of coal merchants W.J. Hawkins, who were there when the station was open. This whole scene has now completely vanished, and has been replaced by Vale Park Drive. (*M. Sale*)

Hazell's Club in Britannia Street, 1968. The club was here until March 1967, when the building was bought by Marks & Spencer so that it could extend its store. Hazell's Club then moved to the sports ground in Victoria Park. Also seen here is one of the original Victorian houses that used to belong to a terrace lining this road. The houses have gone now and a large office block stands on the site. (*M. Sale*)

A return to more destruction in the town as Exchange Street is widened. Many houses have been flattened to accommodate a second carriageway and also to straighten the road. On the opposite side of the road the White Hart has been refronted to set it back a bit more. Further up the road, where the large old chestnut trees used to be, some new trees have been planted further back from the road. (*M. Sale*)

A view of the construction of phase two of Friars Square, 1968. This particular photograph was taken from the Friars Square offices and in the lower part of the image are the beginnings of the new bus station and the ground floor of Woolworth's new store. This view also illustrates the immense height of the cranes that were used on the site. (*R.J. Johnson*)

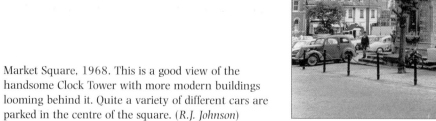

Market Square, 1968. This is a good view of the handsome Clock Tower with more modern buildings looming behind it. Quite a variety of different cars are parked in the centre of the square. (*R.J. Johnson*)

view of the second phase of Friars Square under construction, 1968. The area to the left became the new bus
ation, with the Woolworth's store next to and above it. Stretching from the foreground to the white portacabin
nd van is the original road surface, which became the second carriageway of the covered street. (*R.J. Johnson*)

Friars Square looking towards Market Square, summer 1968. This was the main entrance to the square, and still is although it looks very different now. In the immediate foreground there are now escalators that go down to the Cloisters shopping area. Boots, on the left, moved from here to Hale Leys Shopping Centre in 1982, Argos moved into Boots' former premises. Argos has since moved to Cambridge Close. Just below the Boots sign is the entrance to Jardine's ten-pin bowling centre. (*R.J. Johnson*)

A view of the new roundabout in Walton Street, 1968. Beyond it the new premises of Wilkins Solicitors is being built. Displayed on the scaffolding is the sign of its builders, Webster & Cannon. This firm was responsible for constructing many different buildings in the town as well as further afield. For example, further down Exchange Street is one of its buildings – the former Electricity Board headquarters, which was until recently the planning department of Aylesbury Vale District Council. (*M. Sale*)

The old gas works from the High Street, 1968. The large building on the left is the rear of the Co-op store, and on the right is the rear of the gas showroom which is seen on the following page. In the distance is the car park of the Royal Mail sorting office. As has been mentioned before, this whole area has totally changed with the building of Hampden House and Vale Park Drive. (*M. Sale*)

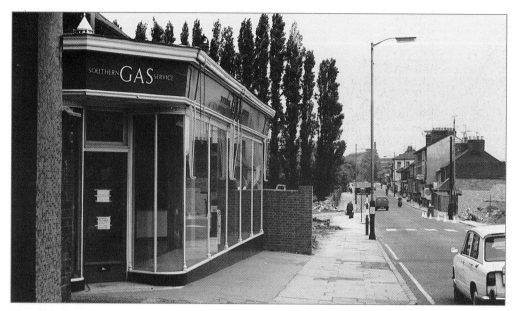

The High Street, 1968. This is a good view of the showroom of Southern Gas. Like many of the buildings in the High Street it has been converted from a Victorian private house; a new part was built on to the front, over the small front garden. A notice on the door tells us that the showroom is now closed and has moved to Friars Square. Opposite the showroom work is under way to widen Exchange Street. (*M. Sale*)

The last act of vandalism in the 1960s – the destruction of the Bulls Head Hotel in Market Square. In 1968 cracks were noticed on the front of the building. It was immediately shored up to stop anything falling off. A contributing factor may have been the demolition of the adjacent Westminster Bank building which could have caused the foundations of the hotel to be undermined. The hotel was closed, and after a while the powers-that-be decided to demolish this 500-year-old building. The saddest thing of all is that the whole site, which covered quite a large area, was cleared. It is hard to believe that all of these buildings were structurally unsafe. But as we have seen throughout this book, nothing stopped the force of 'progress'. (*M. Sale*)

New Street, 1968. Judging by the absence of any cars this photograph must have been taken on a Sunday: even in those days Aylesbury was a very busy place. In the right foreground is the turning for Cambridge Place. Facing us at the end of the street is the Nags Head pub, which is now a memory, as New Street has been widened and a new road now goes through the site of the old pub. (*M. Sale*)

Another view of New Street, 1968. A house is being demolished on the corner of Alexander Road. It was pulled down to create more parking spaces for the Telephone Exchange, which is immediately behind it. On the left are the premises of builders Fleet & Roberts. Today this building has been put to a very different use – it is a Chinese restaurant called Eat As Much As You Like. (*M. Sale*)

This building stood in George Street, and could easily be confused with the entrance to the King's Head. To give some idea of where the photograph was taken note the gates opposite – they are at the rear of the Queen's Head. This little courtyard, photographed in 1968, belonged to a range of buildings that housed the Court School of Dancing and the bookmakers Jock Bezant. (*M. Sale*)

Another photograph of the buildings in the photograph above, showing how old this area was. At the top of the steps is the headquarters of the taxi firm, R.A. Tax. It is doubtful that the car seen here is one of their taxis as it has no wheels. These buildings were demolished in the early 1970s to make way for an office block called Regent House. (*M. Sale*)

Looking towards Friars Square from Temple Street, 1968. This view remained much the same for the following two decades until the shopping centre's revamp in 1991. The man seen leaving the square has just come out of the passage that was at the rear of Boots the Chemist. The little road at the end that goes across the truncated Silver Street follows the same line as Silver Lane. Everything else has completely vanished forever under Friars Square. Those old roads now only exist in old photographs and in the memories of the people who lived and worked there. Even the old Friars Square that is seen here is just a memory. (*M. Sale*)

A view of the bottom of the High Street, 1969, before the roundabout was put in. To accommodate these road 'improvements' many of the Edwardian houses on the left were demolished, together with the war memorial of printers Hazell Watson & Viney. Their factory buildings dominated this end of the High Street and Tring Road, which was locally known as Hazell's Corner. The printing firm closed in 1996 and the buildings were demolished. Part of the site is now occupied by a Tesco supermarket. (*M. Sale*)

ACKNOWLEDGEMENTS

While compiling this book I have had lots of encouragement and help from many people. In particular I would like to thank Peggy Sale who has allowed me to use a good proportion of her photograph collection which features lots of excellent views of Aylesbury in the 1960s. It is a fact that this book would not have been possible without her photographs. Also, I would like to thank the staff at the Local Studies section of the County Library for the use of their facilities. I have spent many hours in there working on this book and the material I have looked through has been extremely useful.

My thanks also go to Richard J. Johnson and David Bailey for their knowledge and advice and for the use of some of Mr Johnson's photographs. Also to Mr Powell, Mr Fountain, Mr Grant, Mr West, Barbara Thorpe and Liz Atkinson for the loan of their pictures. The *Bucks Herald* should also get a mention as its staff have at various times helped with requests for photographs and information regarding the 1960s. I must also thank everyone at Kall Kwik Printing for their encouragement over the last year and a half, and lastly my family for their help and support.